W9-BMN-887

The Life and Times of

PYTHAGORAS

Mitchell Lane
PUBLISHERS

P.O. Box 196
Hockessin, Delaware 19707

BIOGRAPHY FROM

ANCIENT CIVILIZATIONS
LEGENDS, FOLKLORE, AND STORIES OF ANCIENT WORLDS

Titles
in the Series

The Life and Times of

The Life and Times of

PYTHAGORAS

Susan Sales Harkins and William H. Harkins

Printing   1   2   3   4   5   6   7   8   9

Library of Congress Cataloging-in-Publication Data
Harkins, Susan Sales.
  The life and times of Pythagoras / by Susan Sales Harkins and William H. Harkins.
    p. cm. — (Biography from ancient civilizations)
  Includes bibliographical references and index.
  ISBN 978-1-58415-545-4 (library bound)
  1. Pythagoras—Juvenile literature. 2. Philosophers—Greece—Biography—Juvenile literature. I. Harkins, William H. II. Title.
  B243.H37 2008
  182'.2—dc22
  [B]

                                                          2007023492

ABOUT THE AUTHORS: Susan and Bill Harkins live in Kentucky, where they enjoy writing together for children. Susan has written many books for adults and children. Bill is a history buff, who particularly enjoys the Greek classics. In addition to writing, he is a member of the Kentucky Air National Guard.

PHOTO CREDITS: Cover, pp. 1, 3—Raffaello Sanzio; p. 6—Ricardo Andre Frantz; p. 9—BlingBling10; pp. 13, 15, 16, 38—© Jupiter Images; pp. 28, 32, 36—Jonathan Scott; p. 17—ArchyTech; p. 18—Zeichner Galilea; p. 24—A. Hartwell

PUBLISHER'S NOTE: This story is based on the authors' extensive research, which they believe to be accurate. Documentation of such research is contained on page 46. The stories in the Biography From Ancient Civilizations series take place before the invention of photography. Therefore, no accurate images of the people exist. Some artists' engravings, sculptures, and sketches have survived time. Some of the images we have chosen to include may have been modified or colored for artistic purposes only.

   The internet sites referenced herein were active as of the publication date. Due to the fleeting nature of some web sites, we cannot guarantee they will all be active when you are reading this book.

                                                          PLB

The Life and Times of

PYTHAGORAS

                 *For Your Information

In central Greece, the barren peak of Mount Parnassus overlooks olive groves and Delphi. According to Greek mythology, the mountain was sacred to Apollo and the Muses.

CHAPTER
ONE

AN AGE OF GENIUS

Mnesarchus dropped from his horse and handed the reigns to a servant. He took a moment to wipe the beads of sweat from his brow. Shielding his eyes from the sun, he saw a long line waiting outside the temple. The line to see the Pythian oracle was always long. It is good to be rich, he thought. A bag of coins would buy his way to the front of the line.

Far down the mountainside, bright dots of sun sprinkled the blue sea. Overhead loomed the snow-topped peaks of Mount Parnassus. He never tired of standing between mortals and the gods in this holy place. Suddenly, he remembered his mission and headed straight for the temple. He had a date with an oracle.

Moments later, he started down the stone staircase that led to the oracle's chamber. Sweet, refreshing air wafted up and cooled his face. In the torchlit room, he waited quietly on a bench. Behind a thin curtain, the shadow of the oracle sat motionless. She murmured quietly, but he couldn't understand her. One never knew what to expect from the oracle.

It wasn't often that he had time to just sit, and his mind wandered. He was far from his childhood home in Phoenicia. The citizens of Samos had rewarded him with citizenship after he provided food during a drought.

His eyelids began to droop and suddenly, his mind was full of the soft, lovely face of Parthenis. He loved his Greek wife and their home on Samos.

Time and again, business carried him far from home, and he was often lonely. What would his Phoenician family think if they could see him sitting in the dark waiting for a Greek oracle to reveal his future? he wondered.

A movement in the room brought him back to the present. There, by his side, stood a slender priestess. It was time to tell the oracle why he'd come. Just as he opened his mouth to speak, the oracle thrust out her hand and spoke, "Your voyage will be satisfying and profitable. Your wife is pregnant and will give birth to a child surpassing all others in beauty and wisdom, who will be of the greatest benefit to the human race in all aspects of life."[1]

Mnesarchus was stunned. Before he could speak, the priestess was gone. He never did ask a question of the oracle that day.

This child must be exceptional indeed, he thought. The gods obviously thought so because they sent the message unasked.

From that day forward, to honor the oracle Pythia, Mnesarchus called his wife Pythias. When the child the oracle foretold was born, they named him Pythagoras.

Pythagoras (puh-THAH-guh-rus) entered the world at an exciting time. Dictators ruled rival city-states, and gods plagued the common man. However, just a few decades before Pythagoras was born, the world shifted. It was as if the earth had tilted on its axis, pouring logic and wisdom from the skies. The truth was, a few men were turning the world upside down. Not literally, of course—a few brilliant thinkers were changing the way people thought about themselves and the world in which they lived. The change was nothing short of historic. Mankind was claiming the right to control its destiny, and the world would never be the same.

Greeks began to view their gods as more than just immortal humans with huge egos and bad habits. The superhuman brats who meddled in their lives were now seen as supernatural beings of goodness and compassion. Later, Pythagoras would live to see the birth of the first Western democracy, in Athens.

Some historians believe that Mnesarchus and Parthenis were in Sidon, Phoenicia, when Pythagoras was born. Most claim the Greek island of Samos is his birthplace. Regardless of where he was born, he was raised as a Greek in Samos.

Although we don't know the exact date, Pythagoras was probably born around 560 BCE (many sources say 580 BCE). Traditional stories claim he was born on the small Greek island of Samos. Some historians believe Pythagoras was born in Sidon in Phoenicia.[2]

His Phoenician father, Mnesarchus, was a wealthy merchant. His Greek mother, Parthenis, was a descendant of the gods, according to Apollonius of Tyana. This first-century Greek teacher and philosopher was the first to write of Parthenis' claim to the gods. In fact, he was the first to mention Parthenis at all. We don't know who she was or what her real name was. Most likely, Apollonius invented her.[3]

If Pythagoras was born in Samos, Mnesarchus may have kept Greek tradition by hanging a huge wreath of olives over the main door. (When the new child was a girl, the parents hung a wreath of wool.) It's likely that Mnesarchus danced around the house naked, carrying

The Rosicrucian Order, a modern philosophical organization with origins in ancient Egypt, uses a likeness of Pythagoras in its official symbol.

the newborn baby, as was the Greek custom. Friends and family sent gifts to welcome the new child.

Pythagoras had a privileged childhood. According to tradition, his mother came from the island's most aristocratic family—its founders. Most Samians believed the founders were gods, so that made Pythagoras and his mother the descendants of gods.

Like most Greek children, Pythagoras spent his early years at home with his mother. Their courtyard was a lively place where he played, ate, learned his first lessons, and listened to his mother tell stories. He grew up on fables of Greek gods and heroes such as Odysseus. In this inner sanctuary, Pythagoras was safe and well cared for. During his first years, his mother was the most influential person in his life.

Parthenis probably spent most of her time at home tending her children and running her household. Because Mnesarchus was wealthy, his wife had the best of everything. She wore the finest linen tunics. Her house was filled with luxurious furniture. Her family ate off silver (and possibly even gold) plates. Each morning, a personal slave curled or braided her long hair, using silver bands and combs to keep it in place.

Most Greek boys started school at the age of six. They learned philosophy, athletics, music, and painting. In the early part of the sixth century BCE, Greeks put little emphasis on math and science.

Pythagoras was lucky to grow up during a time of relative peace. Often, he traveled to ports along the Mediterranean Sea with his father. It's easy to imagine a young Pythagoras and his father studying the stars from the bow of a sailing ship.

Socially, he was at a disadvantage because of his heritage. Because his father wasn't Greek, neither was he. The people of Samos never considered Pythagoras a true Greek.[4]

Some historians believe that Pythagoras traveled as a teenager to the island of Syros to escape Polycrates, a tyrant. In Syros, he may have studied music with Pherecydes. An early philosopher, Pherecydes used myths to teach his views of creation. According to two ancient writers, Cicero (106 BCE–43 BCE) and St. Augustine (354 CE–430 CE), Pherecydes was the first to teach that the human soul is immortal.[5] Pherecydes believed that the human soul traveled from one body to another, through many lifetimes. Pythagoras would later teach this concept himself, calling it transmigration of the soul.

Scholars and historians debate whether Pythagoras actually studied with Pherecydes. The ancient biographers Duris of Samos and Iamblichus claim that he did.[6]

Some historians contradict their writings, noting, "The fact that Pherecydes taught doctrines . . . involving the soul, made him a suitable teacher to attribute to Pythagoras."[7] In many traditional stories, Pythagoras performs miracles. Some historians believe that ancient writers concocted the relationship with Pherecydes to support the truth of these stories. It's important to note that no one really knows. There are no known contemporary documents connecting Pythagoras and Pherecydes.

Ancient biographers claim that Pythagoras traveled to Miletus in Anatolia (modern-day Turkey) after his father died. On the cusp of manhood (he was just eighteen), Pythagoras would have found the city very different from Samos. The first Greek philosophical movement, known as the Ionian or Milesian school, was well under way there.

By tradition, Pythagoras sought out the most revolutionary minds to teach him: Thales and Anaximander. Both of these philosophers believed that we learn everything through experience and observation. They repeatedly tested their theories—just believing that something was true wasn't enough. Today, we call this system of testing for proof the empirical method. Modern scientists still use this method, and therefore, we credit Thales and Anaximander for being the world's first scientists.

What Pythagoras learned during his travels put him at odds with his countrymen. Greeks believed that their gods controlled everything, and that man simply wasn't capable of understanding the gods. Therefore, people didn't seek answers to explain the world around them. Truthfully, they didn't even ask the questions. They believed they were at the mercy of their gods.

Some modern scholars believe there was no relationship between Pythagoras and these revolutionary philosophers.[8] Thales was a remarkable thinker who founded the Ionian movement. During his lifetime, he wrote five mathematical theorems. Using geometry, he determined the size of the sun and the moon. According to Herodotus, an ancient historian who lived from 484 BCE to 425 BCE, Thales predicted a solar eclipse. Decades later, Plato included Thales in his list of Seven Sages of Greece (men Plato considered wiser than all others).

In contrast, Pythagoras was just a rich Greek boy. Although Pythagoras received an exceptional education, he wasn't a revolutionary thinker—not yet. It is hard to imagine Thales, the "Father of Science," taking on a teenager such as Pythagoras as a student. There's no way to know for certain whether he did or not. However, many historians and modern scientists think Thales and Anaximander did indeed influence Pythagoras. Like the Ionians,

Although no one knows what Pythagoras looked like, he wore a long beard, which was contrary to the Greek style of his time.

Pythagoras studied the cosmos and mathematics. In addition, both Thales and Pythagoras never drank wine, which was unusual in ancient Greece.

Eventually, Pythagoras left Miletus. Traditional stories claim that Thales sent him to Memphis, Egypt, to study geometry and Egyptian. Pythagoras stayed there almost twenty years and may even have become an Egyptian priest, which would explain his later views on the human soul. According to Egyptians, the soul lives after the body dies. Greeks had no such concept. Scholars also believe that the Egyptians introduced Pythagoras to astronomy.

Whether Pythagoras really lived in Egypt and became a priest isn't known. The ancient writer Isocrates claimed that Pythagoras visited Egypt, but later admitted that the Egyptian story was fiction. Despite this admission, many of Isocrates' contemporaries accepted the story as fact. Subsequent writers included the Egyptian trip, and in fact, modern historians still do.[9] The number of conflicting stories further confuse the truth. According to J.A. Phillip, "Antiphon . . . tells how Polycrates gave Pythagoras a letter of introduction to Amasis, how he then acquired the language of Egypt, and finally penetrated the priestly secrets. . . . The Cambyses episode elaborated on by Iamblichus carries him to Babylonia . . . Porphyry has him visit Delos on his way to Italy . . . Diogenes Laertius has him descend with Epimenides into the Idaean cave."[10]

The traditional stories go on to say that Pythagoras was taken prisoner in a war. After King Cambyses II of Persia (modern-day Iran) attacked Egypt in about 525 BCE, Pythagoras traveled with other Egyptian priests to Babylon as captives. Pythagoras continued his studies with the magi (Babylonian priests) and for twelve years, he studied religion, mathematics, music, and astrology. Most likely, it was in Babylon that he learned the theorem that today we call the Pythagorean Theorem.[11]

At the time, Babylonians used a number system based on the number 60. (Today, we use a base-10 numbering system.) They were expert astronomers for their time and predicted earthly events using the positions of the planets. Today we call this practice astrology. Some people still practice it, but the scientific community no longer pursues astrology as a science.

Pythagoras spent over thirty years studying in Egypt and Babylon, according to stories from writers who lived hundreds of years after Pythagoras. Yet Aristotle, the first ancient writer to document Pythagoras' life, never mentioned either of these voyages.[12]

Most modern historians and scholars depend on six ancient writers when studying Pythagoras. Aristoxenus of Tarentum, Dicaearchus of Messana, and Timaeus of Tauromenium wrote about the famous mathematician and his followers during the fourth and third centuries BCE. Diogenes Laertius, Porphyry, and Iamblichus wrote much later, in the second and third centuries CE. Iamblichus

Renaissance artists represented Pythagoras in contemporary scenes. In this woodcut, Pythagoras uses a counting table to compete against Roman philosopher Boethius, who uses algorithms.

seems to be the traditional storyteller and the most often quoted, and his work is full of miracles, myths, and contradictions. Aristoxenus of Tarentum was a student of Aristotle and claimed to know members of the last colony of Pythagoreans.

It is important to note that none of these men wrote from firsthand knowledge of Pythagoras or his school. As Walter Burkert says, "One is tempted to say that there is not a single detail in the life of Pythagoras that stands uncontradicted. It is possible, from a more or less critical selection of the data, to construct a plausible account; but it is bound to rest on shaky foundations, for no documentary evidence has appeared."[13]

Pythagoras may not have studied in Egypt or Babylon. However, in the sixth century BCE, the Greeks began to study and apply mathematical principles that the Egyptians and Babylonians had been

The Pythagoreans were a secretive society. Higher mathematics were taught only to the innermost circle of students, the mathematikoi.

using for centuries. We credit Pythagoras with introducing these concepts to the ancient Western world. For this, he became a legend, even in his own time.

It was easy for Greeks to believe Pythagoras was divine, given his mother's standing in Samian society. One legend claimed he was the son of the god Apollo and the virgin Pythias (his mortal mother). It didn't matter that his mother had a husband and possibly even two sons when she gave birth to Pythagoras.

None of Pythagoras' writings survive to help separate myths like this one from his real life. The people who wrote about him had to rely on traditional stories.

The Greek Island of Samos

The Greek island of Samos lies off the coast of modern-day Turkey in the Aegean Sea. Vineyards dot the fertile landscape: Samos was, and still is, famous for its fine wines.

In ancient times, the island was a center of Ionian culture and luxury. Ionia is an ancient coastal region on the Aegean Sea, off the western coast of modern-day Turkey. Merchants traveling from Asia Minor to the west stopped at the island's busy port.

The city was known for its public works and its school. Their sculptors, metalworkers, and engineers were highly acclaimed throughout Greece and Asia Minor. Sometime in the sixth century BCE, Samians built a huge aqueduct to supply fresh water to the capital. The ruling tyrant, Polycrates, hired an engineer named Eupalinos to manage the project. To construct the aqueduct, two groups of workers dug from both sides and met in the middle of the mountain. Tourists still visit the aqueduct today.

Eupalinian aqueduct
Samos, Greece

According to tradition, Samos was settled by Greeks long before Pythagoras was born. As the story goes, the Pythian oracle told Ancaeus, a descendant of Zeus, to colonize a small island. Being one of the wisest men of his time, Ancaeus obeyed the oracle. Many companions from Athens, Epidaurus, and Chalcis went with him. Their sacrifices were great, but by the sixth century BCE, the island of Samos was well established and thriving. When Pythagoras was born, Ancaeus' descendants still lived on the island, and the locals considered them divine. Since Parthenis, Pythagoras' mother, descended from Ancaeus, Pythagoras was therefore, by tradition, also the descendant of gods.

Historians are not sure who really settled Samos, but they believe people from Epidaurus, a small Greek city near the Saronic Gulf, might have migrated to the island. By the seventh century BCE, Samos was so successful it became part of the Ionian League, a confederacy of twelve Ionian cities that met for festivals and athletic competitions.

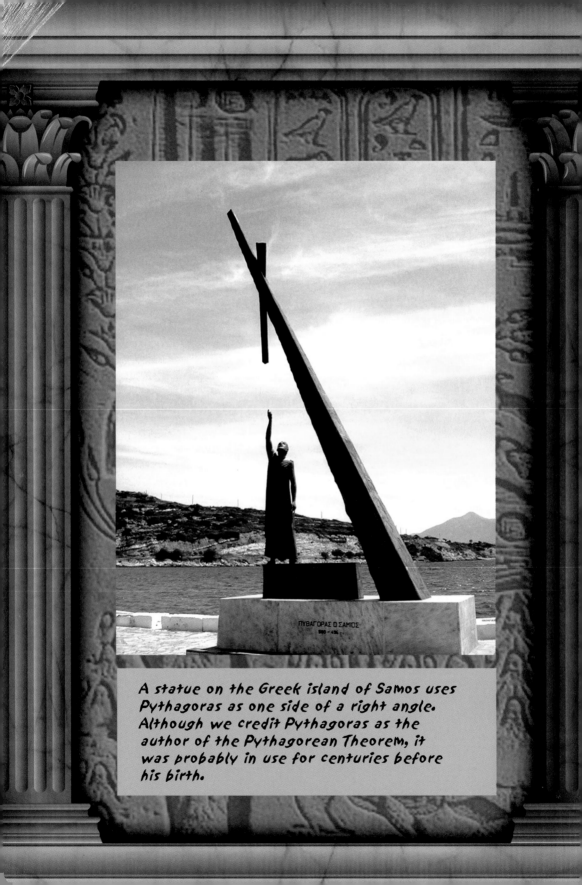

A statue on the Greek island of Samos uses Pythagoras as one side of a right angle. Although we credit Pythagoras as the author of the Pythagorean Theorem, it was probably in use for centuries before his birth.

CHAPTER
TWO

THE PYTHAGOREAN SCHOOL

If traditional stories are correct, Pythagoras studied abroad for thirty years. At age fifty, he returned to Samos and began his own school. He was still a misfit among the Samians. He never cut his hair or beard, and he wore trousers rather than traditional Greek clothing.[1]

Little is known about his first school, which he called the Semicircle. As a group, Pythagoras and his students lived simply. In an effort to remain pure, they didn't eat meat or fish or drink wine. Nor did they wear wool or leather.

Philosophy and mathematics were their main pursuits. In both areas, Pythagoreans were revolutionary. Numbers held spiritual meaning for Pythagoras. They were much more than just symbols that represented numeric values. Furthermore, he believed that a mathematical equation was also a spiritual question.

Unfortunately for Pythagoras, the Greeks of Samos hadn't changed much in the thirty years he'd been away. They still weren't as interested in mathematics as they were in philosophy and music. Numbers were just symbols to Greeks—solving math problems certainly wasn't a religious experience for them. However, the Samians respected Pythagoras. They often turned to him for advice on politics and social issues. This left Pythagoras with less time to teach.

Eventually, Pythagoras left Samos. Traditional stories claim that he held no interest in politics; he just wanted to study and teach. As he traveled, he met people who knew about him and his school. Still, finding a new home was hard, until he visited Croton, a Greek colony in southern Italy. As his ship approached the Croton harbor, he saw a crowd on shore. When he stepped off the boat, the crowd cheered. Pythagoras was shocked to learn that they were waiting to see him!

According to Porphyry in the *Life of Pythagoras*, the Crotonians welcomed Pythagoras warmly: "When Pythagoras set foot in Italy and arrived in Croton, he was received as a man of remarkable powers and experience after his many travels and as someone well supplied by fortune with regard to his personal characteristics. For his manner was grand and liberal, and in his voice, his character and everything else about him there was grace and harmony in abundance."[2] However, because Porphyry wrote about Pythagoras several hundred years after his death, we don't really know how the Crotonians received him.

Soon after arriving in Croton, Pythagoras gave several speeches to the citizens. Most likely, he hoped to establish a school and needed their support. Before the first speech, however, he performed one of his famous miracles. On the road, he met a group of fishermen and claimed to know the exact number of fish each had caught. When the men counted their fish, he was right. Pythagoras then asked the men to return the fish to the sea, which they did. By the time Pythagoras gave his first speech, this feat was well known.

The text of Pythagoras' speeches no longer exists. Iamblichus recorded four, but he did so centuries after the fact. There's no way to determine if Pythagoras even gave the speeches, let alone what he really said.

Pythagoras stayed in Croton and built a new school. Just as in Samos, he taught in secrecy. Knowledge was dangerous in the wrong hands, or so he thought. Pythagoras believed that gaining knowledge was an attempt to be closer to the gods. He also believed that the human soul developed over many lifetimes until it reached a divine state. The only way to reach the highest level was to devote one's life to learning.

Once someone decided to join the school, the hopeful student spent a lot of time with Pythagoras. Mostly, Pythagoras wanted to know how well this person treated his friends and family. Next, he tested potential students on their ability to learn.

The lucky students that made it into Pythagoras' inner circle of *mathematikoi* ("mathematicians") donated everything they owned to the communal society. Worldly possessions only distracted one's soul, and a distracted soul couldn't learn. Both men and women were admitted into his school. Greeks didn't educate girls, so allowing women into the school was radical. For the next five years, the novice didn't speak, having taken a vow of silence. Pythagoras believed that anyone who could meet the requirements had the self-control necessary to learn.

At the end of the five years of silence, Pythagoras admitted the student fully into the society. Usually the students concentrated on one of four subjects: mathematics, music, geometry, and philosophy. Often, their studies overlapped.

Students who couldn't meet the demands were expelled. The student received twice the value of whatever property they had donated to the society when they joined. It is believed that from then on, the Pythagoreans refused to acknowledge the failed student. They even erected a tombstone to show that the student was dead to them.

About five hundred *mathematikoi* lived at the school. They lived, ate, exercised, studied, socialized, and worshiped together. In truth, these students were more than students: They were Pythagoras' disciples. They didn't marry, although some ancient writings refer to Pythagoras' wife and daughters. It's impossible to know whether he had a family.

Other students called the *akousmatikoi* ("listeners") never saw Pythagoras. A huge veil separated them from their teacher and the *mathematikoi*. When the *akousmatikoi* were present, Pythagoras taught in parables and enigmas. Because the *mathematikoi* knew the true meanings of specific words and phrases, they were able to grasp the full meaning behind the lessons.

According to ancient writers, one such lesson was "Abstain from beans." This statement eventually evolved into the mistaken belief that Pythagoreans thought beans were divine! There's even a myth that Pythagoras faced a violent mob, which killed him when he refused to run across a bean field to escape.

The real meaning is probably political. In ancient times, citizens voted by placing beans in jars. Pythagoras was warning his followers to avoid political affairs. Specifically, he warned them not to take sides in a civil war or any other violent uprising.[3]

As students, the *akousmatikoi* led normal lives. They had jobs, families, and even held political office. However, they were never allowed to learn the most sacred teachings, such as higher mathematics.

Pythagoreans lived simply, not poorly. They shared everything, including their money, property, and clothing. They considered luxury a distraction, but they lived comfortably. Each day was carefully planned. After waking up, they remained in bed, spending a few moments recalling the previous day's events and planning the day ahead. After rising, they walked alone. Then, they met to greet one another and make an offering to the gods.

After lunch, small groups walked together to discuss lessons. In the afternoon, they bathed. In the evening, they ate dinner together. Their day ended with readings and religious rituals. As they fell asleep, they thought about the day they were leaving behind.

We know little about the actual lessons Pythagoras taught. There are no contemporary writings from either of his schools, nor did Pythagoras leave any writings of his own. Almost one hundred years after his death, a few followers began to write about the school and their beliefs. Historians are forced to piece together what little we know of Pythagoras and his teachings from these writings.

Croton

Achaeans from Peloponnese (Greece) founded the colony of Croton, in Magna Graecia, around 710 BCE. Magna Graecia was the ancient region of southern Italy colonized by Greeks. In ancient times, the town flourished. By the time Pythagoras moved to Croton, the city was already well known for its athletes.

A few Croton Pythagoreans became quite famous in their own right. Alcmaeon of Croton was an early medical writer and philosopher. Philolaus was a philosopher, mathematician, and astronomer.

Hannibal of Carthage

The remains of an ancient Greek castle, Le Castella, stand as a reminder to the town's long and varied history. The foundation is Greek, but the main structure, what's left of it, is medieval. Originally, the castle was a series of towers and walls that enclosed a small village. The Greeks built this small community on an island. A narrow land bridge connects the island to the coast, making it accessible only by foot. There's a legend that the famous Carthaginian military commander Hannibal camped on the island after retreating from Rome in 204 BCE. The Romans then established a small settlement there named Castra.

Over the next several centuries, Croton fell to many rulers, most notably the Romans. In 870 CE, the Saracens (invaders who were of Arabic descent) sacked the entire area. Their victory was particularly bloody.

A century later, Otto II of the Holy Roman Empire tried to drive out the Saracens, but he was unsuccessful. Eventually, the Normans did what Otto couldn't. (The Normans were originally from Scandinavia, but by this time, they ruled large areas of Europe.) By 1861, Cotrone (as they called it then) was part of the Kingdom of Italy. In 1928, the citizens changed the town's name to Crotone.

A. Hartwell del.   Pendleton Lith.

PYTHAGORAS.

Most of Pythagoras' teachings were radical in his time. Today, they are part of our scientific foundation.

CHAPTER THREE

PYTHAGOREAN PHILOSOPHY

Pythagoras is believed to be the first person to refer to himself as a philosopher. Literally, a philosopher is someone who loves wisdom. As a philosopher and a teacher, Pythagoras was open to all knowledge, even the study of religion. However, his belief in numbers was the cornerstone of everything he believed. Numbers were the essence of existence, he thought. Numbers could answer all questions about the human soul, nature, and the cosmos. In other words, numbers could reveal all knowledge.

According to Pythagoras, the human soul had three parts: reason, emotion, and intelligence. He also believed that the human soul is immortal, which was a radical idea for Greeks at that time. When the body dies, he believed, its soul transmigrates (moves) into another body. Today, we call this reincarnation.

Pythagoras even claimed to remember past lives he had led. According to tradition, Pythagoras claimed to be Euphorbus of the *Iliad* by Homer.[1] While visiting Argos, Pythagoras saw a shield from Troy and burst into tears. He said the shield was his in a past life, but no one believed him. He then told people to check inside the shield, where they would find his name, Euphorbus, inscribed. When they took down the shield, they found the inscription, just as he'd said they would.[2] Of course, there's no way to know whether the story is true.

Separating Pythagorean philosophy from numbers is nearly impossible because numbers occur naturally in almost every subject. For instance, Pythagoras believed that each person is reincarnated every 216 years, which is the number 6 cubed (6 x 6 x 6). In this case, 216 represents repetition.

Greeks resisted Pythagoras' ideas on the human soul. They believed in just one life. After the body died, the soul went to Hades (the Underworld) and stayed there. Only gods could leave Hades.

By dismissing Hades, the Pythagoreans created a new question: Where do human souls live when they're not trapped inside a physical body? To answer this, Pythagoras created two worlds. According to him, humans live in a limited and temporary world. They are limited by their physical experience as humans. Their souls, however, exist in an unlimited world—the same world in which the gods live. Pythagoras taught that the unlimited world, the world of the divine, is real and endless.

Gods were important to the Pythagoreans. Above all the other gods, they honored Apollo, the god of the sun, music, art, medicine, prophecy, and philosophy. They used numbers to determine which days to worship. They entered their temple from the right side, which allowed them to symbolically enter the unlimited world. They left the temple from the left side, to reenter the limited world. They didn't cremate the bodies of their dead, because they believed that flames belonged to the unlimited world and were sacred. Limited-world bodies should never mix with the unlimited world.

Numbers influenced the study of the cosmos. According to Pythagoras, the universe consists of ten spheres: the sun, the moon, Earth, Mercury, Venus, Mars, Jupiter, Saturn, the counter-Earth, and the central hearth. The invisible central hearth is the center of the universe. Everything comes from this sphere. The counter-Earth can't be seen from Earth because it's on the opposite side of the central hearth.

The idea that Earth was a sphere was new to the ancient Greeks. Most of them, including Thales, the first scientist, believed that the world was a flat mass of land floating in a giant sea.

Two centuries after Pythagoras said that Earth was a sphere, Aristotle watched the shadow Earth cast on the moon during a lunar eclipse. The shadow cast the arc of a circle. In studying the stars, Aristotle noticed that they moved as he traveled north or south. If one traveled far enough, whole constellations disappeared below the horizon. According to Aristotle, this is exactly what would happen if one were walking on the surface of a sphere.

Around 280 BCE, Aristarchus, a Greek astronomer, calculated the approximate size of the moon. He used the size of the lunar shadow's arc, plus the known rules of geometry. Considering his limited technology, he was amazingly close. He said that the moon is about one-third the size of Earth. Today, we know that the moon is closer to one-fourth the size of Earth.

A few decades later, Eratosthenes computed the size of Earth. To do so, he measured the shadows cast by two sticks stuck in the ground at noon of the summer solstice. A stick in Syene, Egypt, didn't cast a shadow, because that city lies on the equator and the sun was directly overhead. A stick in Alexandria, Egypt, cast a slight shadow. Eratosthenes used the distance between the two cities and the degree of the cast shadow in Alexandria to determine Earth's circumference. Remarkably, his answer was within 15 percent of the Earth's actual circumference (which is approximately 24,900 miles). A few centuries later, during the second century CE, Hipparchus calculated the distance from Earth to the moon as 240,000 miles. He was extremely close to the actual 238,855 miles.

To Pythagoras, Earth was more than just a round rock hanging in space. Some of his ideas on the cosmos were mystical. He believed that all the heavenly bodies followed mathematical patterns and specific ratios that match the musical scale. As these bodies fly through space, they produce music that only a few humans can hear. The faster

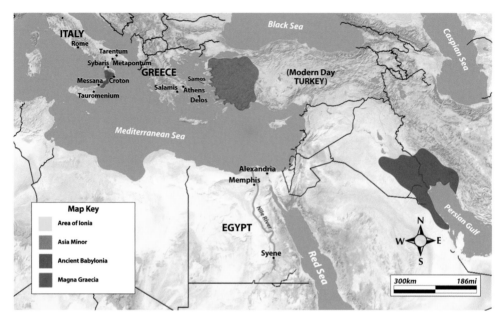

According to tradition, Pythagoras was well traveled. He returned home to Samos after living for more than thirty years in Babylon and Egypt.

a sphere moves, the higher the pitch it plays. In fact, the Greek word *cosmos* means "harmony." Pythagoras claimed he could hear the music of the spheres.

Music was more than entertainment for the Pythagoreans; it was part of their spiritual life. Music could heal. Furthermore, the right music—namely, stringed instruments—promoted good health. The Pythagoreans even played specific tunes to make themselves feel better. They didn't play or use wind instruments because they believed the music of those instruments hurt the soul.

Pythagoras' contribution to the world of music is far more important than a few mystical tunes. We credit him with discovering the musical scale that we still use today.

According to legend, Pythagoras heard music in an ancient market. It's easy to imagine Pythagoras walking in the morning sun, before it was too hot. Most likely, he brushed against other shoppers and examined the fruit for sale. Perhaps he stopped to admire the workmanship on a pair of sandals.

Mingling with the pleasant smells of fresh fruits and breads was the ever-present smell of hay and manure from the livestock. Perhaps more invasive than the unpleasant smells of so many people and animals in one place was the constant clamor of voices, competing to be heard. Tradesmen and shoppers bickered over prices. Jewelry and coins jingled. Goats bleated, chickens clucked, servants gossiped, and children cried for their lunch and naps.

It would have been hard for Pythagoras to hear music in all that din, but by tradition, that's exactly what happened. Through all the normal noise of a busy ancient market, Pythagoras heard the hammers of a blacksmith. Instead of the clangs and clanks that everyone else heard and ignored, Pythagoras heard music. The blacksmith hammers produced sounds that were pleasing to his ear.

Always in pursuit of knowledge, Pythagoras stepped inside the blacksmith shop. From the blacksmith, he learned that the smith's hammers weighed six, eight, nine, and twelve pounds. When pounding iron, these hammers produced different sounds. Pounding at the same time, the hammers produced a musical consonance.

He began experimenting on a monochord, an ancient musical instrument with only one string. Pressing on the string at certain positions produced specific notes. By experimenting with the positions, Pythagoras developed the theory of musical ratios.

According to this theory, each musical note has a unique frequency, which equals the number of times the sound vibrates in a given period. The ratio between the frequencies of two different notes determines the degree of consonance between the two notes when played together. The lower the ratio, the more consonant the notes are and the better the two notes sound together.

Pythagoras didn't have the technology to measure a note's frequency. Instead, he measured the string used to produce the note. He found a relationship between the length of the string and the sound the string produced. The shorter the string, the faster the vibration. Higher vibrations produced higher tones. When the frequency of notes correspond to one another mathematically, they sound good played together.

The lowest ratio is written as 1:1, which represents the same note, or multiple notes in unison. By pressing the monochord's string in the middle, Pythagoras produced the same note, only an octave higher. For instance, if an unpressed string produces the note known as middle C, holding the string down in the exact middle produces C one octave higher than middle C. We can write this ratio as 1:2 because the pressed string vibrates twice as fast. A string twice the length of another will produce the same note an octave *lower*.

Even for the musically inclined, the Pythagorean scale is complex. Interestingly, most of the Western world still uses his eight-note scale: do, re, mi, fa, so, la, ti, do'. Using Pythagoras' ratios, musicians can transpose music from one key to another. Furthermore, musicians can determine whether two notes sound good together by calculating their mathematical ratio. In theory, you can write music by simply arranging ratios.

What can you take from this short discussion? The next time you hear a pleasing musical combination, you'll know that the ratio between the notes must be in whole numbers, mathematically speaking. More importantly, Pythagoras thought of musical notes as numbers. The idea that a person didn't need a musical instrument to write or hear music was revolutionary.

For Pythagoras, the discovery was more than just musical. Music had order, and that order was mathematical. It was proof that his lifelong pursuit—to show that numbers could explain the universe—had merit.

What Happened to Greek Science?

We know that Pythagoras challenged the world when he claimed that Earth, the sun, the moon, and all the planets were spheres floating in space. For the next several centuries, astronomers and mathematicians used this theory to learn more about Earth and the universe. However, the idea that the world was flat persisted.

Early Christians get much of the blame, and it's true that some early Christians considered Greeks pagan—a word used, often negatively, to describe followers of a religion with many gods, and also people who follow no religion at all. Others, such as St. Augustine, wanted to apply Greek knowledge to religious studies.

What we can't ignore is that the Greek scientific community was in trouble before Jesus was born. The "golden age" had passed, and the ancient Greeks were producing few new ideas.[3]

Early Christians were more interested in spiritual development than science. They probably didn't set out to destroy science, but they simply weren't interested. According to Margaret Wertheim, "Christians did not stamp out Greek science; their interest simply lay elsewhere, and meanwhile, the culture that had given rise to this science had itself disintegrated. Greek science died in the West not through persecution but because there weren't enough enthusiastic practitioners to keep the tradition alive."[4]

Hypatia

Toward the end of the fourth century CE, that attitude shifted. There was a revival of Pythagorean thought in Alexandria. At the center of this movement, called Neoplatonism, was a woman named Hypatia (hy-PAY-shuh). Although scientific in nature, the Neoplatonism movement offered an alternative to Christianity.

All that ended when a Christian named Cyril took charge of Alexandria in 412 CE. He was a fanatic and wanted all the Jews and Neoplatonists to leave the city. When Hypatia refused to convert to Christianity, a mob of Christian zealots beat her to death. A contemporary writer claimed the crowd stripped her naked and skinned her alive.[5]

Triangular Numbers

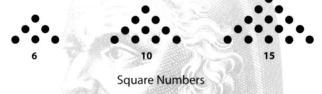

6   10   15

Square Numbers

4   9   16

Combinations

6   6

Pythagoreans gave numbers geometric shapes. By arranging dots that stood for the numbers, they created two-dimensional figures.

CHAPTER
FOUR

THE ESSENCE OF ALL THINGS IS NUMBERS

Pythagoras believed that numbers are real entities, with personalities and characteristics. Odd numbers represent the world of the gods, the divine, and human souls. Even numbers represent the physical world of humans. Odd numbers are male, and represent goodness and the right. Even numbers are female, and represent evil and the left. The number one is both even and odd. The concept of zero did not exist.

For better or worse, the Pythagoreans saw mathematics as a male activity. Women, Pythagoras believed, could study and learn mathematics; however, a woman must draw upon her male element to do so. Just how women accomplished this isn't known. Most likely, they simply applied themselves to their studies, while rejecting the traditional female roles in society.

In modern times, men continue to dominate the field of mathematics. As Margaret Wertheim wrote in 1995, "Although Pythagorean mysticism has long since disappeared, in this respect it has cast a long shadow across Western culture, for even today Mathematical Woman is still struggling to defend herself as a legitimate figure."[1]

Chapter FOUR

The first ten numbers—1, 2, 3, 4, 5, 6, 7, 8, 9, and 10—are sacred in the Pythagorean system. The number 10 is the most sacred number of all. Pythagoras gave each number a name and purpose:

#1 is Monad, the origin of everything.
#2 is Dyad, and represents creation.
#3 is Triad, the first true number.
#4 is Tetrad, and represents completion and justice.
#5 is Pentad, and symbolizes the union of opposites.
#6 is Hexad, and represents health and marriage.
#7 is Heptad, and symbolizes the human body.
#8 is Octad, and symbolizes friendship.
#9 is Ennead, and represents passage.
#10 is Decad, the number of eternity and divinity.

Because numbers were archetypes, they provided insight into human behavior.[2] For Pythagoreans, "mathematics was the key not simply to the physical world, but more importantly to the spiritual world—for they believed that numbers were literally gods. By contemplating numbers and their relationships, the Pythagoreans sought union with the 'divine.' For them, mathematics was first and foremost a religious activity."[3]

Furthermore, Pythagoras saw a relationship between numbers and morality: "The modern separation between mathematics and ethics that we so take for granted would have horrified Pythagoras, who was one of the first to understand that math could be applied to the development of destructive technologies, and hence entails a moral responsibility."[4]

Not only did numbers represent quantities and have characteristics, numbers also represented geometric shapes. Today, we use symbols to represent numbers. Pythagoreans used a series of dots to form lines, triangles, and rectangles. For instance, the numbers 3, 6, 10, and 15 are triangular numbers because you can arrange the dots of each to create a triangle. The numbers 4, 9, and 16 are square numbers for the same reason. The number 12 is a rectangle; 5 is a pentagon. Some numbers, such as 6, have more than one shape. The number 6 is both triangular and rectangular (2 rows of 3 dots).

The Pythagoreans weren't just playing with shapes. Working with these forms, the Pythagoreans discovered a number of complex theorems. Today, we express those theorems using equations, not dots or shapes.

Pythagoras' best-known contribution to mathematics is the Pythagorean Theorem. This theorem states that for any right angle, the sum of the squares of the lengths of the two shorter sides equals the square of the length of the longest side. In other words:

$$a^2 + b^2 = c^2$$

Historians credit Pythagoras and his followers for this basic theorem. The truth is, the Egyptians were using it for centuries before Pythagoras "discovered" it. It's also possible that the Babylonians knew the theorem as early as 1800 BCE. Archaeologists have found cuneiform tablets that support this theory.

Pythagoras gets credit for the theorem because he did more than use it. Pythagoreans worked hard to prove the theorem scientifically. They saw the square as a geometric shape, and they used the square to repeatedly prove the theorem. In other words, a square built on the right triangle's longest side (called the hypotenuse) is equal to the sum of the squares built on the two shorter sides. It's amazing that the Pythagoreans were able to prove this theorem using geometric shapes instead of numbers.

The diagram shown on the next page does a good job of showing how this theorem works. A square is built on each side of the triangle. Using the two smaller squares, a^2 and b^2, you can fill the largest square, c^2.

Pythagorean Theorem

Mathematicians through the centuries have set forth several proofs to demonstrate the Pythagorean Theorem. Around 300 BCE, Greek mathematician Euclid, in his standard geometry reference Elements, *supplied two very different proofs for the theorem. The first proof, Proposition I.47, uses the figure below. It is sometimes called Euclid's Windmill. In 1876, a novel proof using a trapezoid was discovered by James Garfield, later president of the United States, while he was serving in the House of Representatives.*

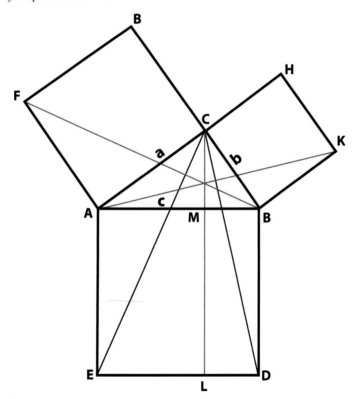

For a right-angled triangle with legs a and b and hypotenuse c, the square on the hypotenuse is equal to the sum of the squares of the sides:

$$a^2 + b^2 = c^2$$

Women Mathematicians

Since ancient times, men have dominated the world of mathematics. Until the twentieth century, few women received formal training in mathematics. Instead, they were taught by male relatives—fathers, uncles, and even brothers.

Hypatia of Alexandria (370 CE–415 CE) was a Greek philosopher, astronomer, and mathematician. She learned math from her father, Theon. She's most famous for leading the Neoplatonic School in Egypt around 400 CE. Her students were both pagan and Christian. According to traditional stories, an enraged mob killed her at the urging of Cyril of Alexandria.

Sophie Germain

Sophie Germain (zhair-MAN) was French (1776–1831). A book on Archimedes sparked her love of math when she was just a child. She corresponded with scholars, but used a man's name for fear they wouldn't take a woman seriously. In 1816, she won a prize for her work on the law of vibrating elastic surfaces. Her work enabled engineers to construct the Eiffel Tower.

Amalie "Emmy" Noether (NUR-ter) was born in Germany in 1882. Her father, a professor of mathematics at the University of Erlangen, taught her. Emmy couldn't enroll at the university because they didn't allow women. In 1902, when the university finally admitted women, Emmy was the only woman there to take math. She worked on Einstein's theory of relativity at the University of Gottingen, but not as an employee. They wouldn't hire her because she was a woman. Eventually, they did hire her, but paid her far less than the men she worked with. Her focus was algebra and she was an expert at abstract concepts. In 1933, the National Socialist Party, led by Adolf Hitler, came to power. Because she was Jewish, she lost her job. She moved to Philadelphia, where she met Albert Einstein. She died in 1935.

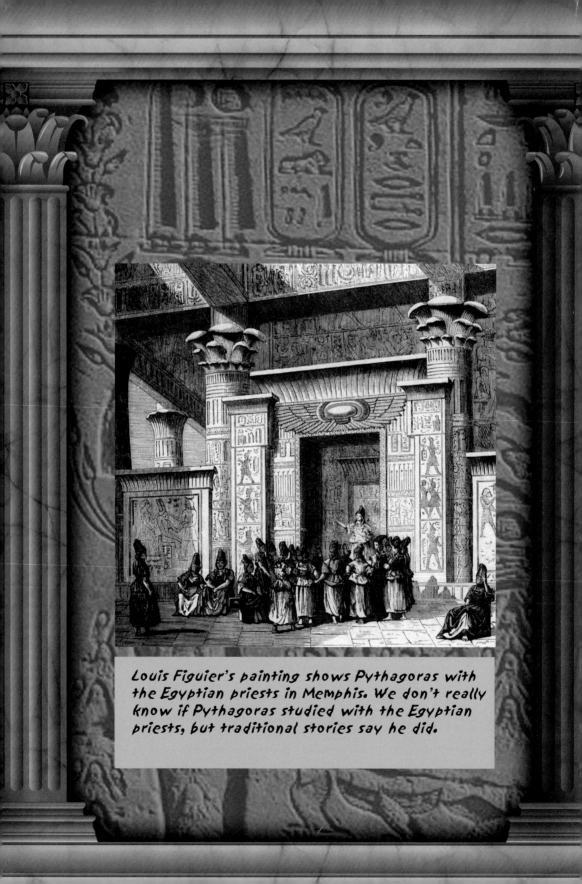

Louis Figuier's painting shows Pythagoras with the Egyptian priests in Memphis. We don't really know if Pythagoras studied with the Egyptian priests, but traditional stories say he did.

CHAPTER
FIVE

HIS FINAL YEARS

Pythagoras lived in Croton for about twenty years. Between 510 and 500 BCE, a violent mob destroyed the school. According to legend, Pythagoras refused to admit Cylon (sometimes spelled Kyon), a wealthy noblemen of Croton, into the school. Pythagoras believed Cylon had a nasty temper. As an act of revenge, Cylon incited the citizens of Croton to attack the school.

Some historians believe that the citizens of Croton were responding to the society's secrecy.[1] Perhaps their anger had more to do with politics. Pythagoras chose students from the aristocracy, young men who were Croton's future leaders. However, it was difficult to become one of Pythagoras' students and even more difficult to remain one. The number of Crotonians whom Pythagoras refused to admit or later expelled grew quickly. Soon, the ruling council was full of Pythagoreans.[2]

Iamblichus writes about a war between Croton and Sybaris. Not everyone agreed with the way the ruling council, full of Pythagoreans, divided the spoils of Croton's victory over Sybaris. By this time, more Greeks were struggling with their political system and demanding reforms. Western democracy was being born.

Chapter FIVE

According to traditional stories, an angry mob set fire to Pythagoras' school with most of the students blocked inside. At least sixty people died in the flames. One traditional story claims Pythagoras' followers threw their bodies into the flames to build a human bridge. Pythagoras then walked over the bodies, over the fire, and escaped. He died of grief soon after.

One of the most curious stories about Pythagoras' death comes from the misunderstanding of his saying, "Abstain from beans." One story says he escaped the fire and ran until he got to a bean field. Because Pythagoreans believed beans to be divine, he refused to enter the field. His pursuers cut his throat on the edge of the field.

Another account says Pythagoras spent the rest of his life wandering Italy. By some accounts, he lived to be nearly one hundred years old. According to Aristotle, Pythagoras knew trouble was coming. He warned his students and then moved to Metapontum (in southern Italy) before the fire.[3]

We don't know when or how Pythagoras died. We do know that he never established another school. According to legend, he hid in the temple of the Muses in Metapontum. No one dared enter the temple to seize him, but Crotonians who followed him to the temple kept his supporters from helping him. He starved to death there.

In addition, it appears that there were two revolts. During a second revolt, angry mobs burned schoolhouses throughout southern Italy.[4] A few survivors struggled to keep the society going, but by 300 BCE, there were no Pythagoreans in Italy.

A few hundred years later, one of the most famous philosophers of all time, Plato, was tutored by a Pythagorean. Plato, like the Pythagoreans, believed that musical ratios guided the heavenly bodies. He also believed in two worlds: the visible and the invisible. His concept was similar to Pythagoras' limited and unlimited dual worlds.

By the second century CE, there were no Pythagorean societies left. However, Pythagoreanism survived as a sort of mystical cult for over a thousand years.[5] Even the early Christian church had a few

Pythagorean thinkers: Roger Bacon (1214–1292) believed that knowledge of language and science led to a better understanding of theology, and Cardinal Nicholas of Cusa (1400–1464) saw god as a mathematical creator.[6]

Nicolaus Copernicus (1473–1543) claimed that the sun was the center of our universe and that Earth orbited the sun. A century later, Johannes Kepler (1571–1630) worked from Pythagoras' teachings in mathematics and astronomy. He called himself a Pythagorean because he believed that a divine being created the universe using mathematical principles. Kepler is most famous for being the first to describe the shape of the planets' orbits around the sun.

Thanks to higher math, as Margaret Wertheim writes, "we have come to believe that we inhabit the third planet of a middle-aged star on the outer edge of a spiral galaxy that is one of millions of galaxies scattered throughout a vast, and possibly infinite, universe. . . . In the modern West, matter, space, and time have all been defined in purely mathematical terms . . . Rather than see ourselves in relation to mythical heroes, gods, and religious laws, we in the West see ourselves now in relation to atoms, stars, and scientific laws."[7]

Today, we remember Pythagoras as a mathematician and one of the first scientists. Historians and scholars tend to disagree, as some think he was a religious fanatic. We don't know whether Pythagoras or his followers originated most of the school's teachings. In fact, we can't even trace Pythagorean beliefs back to Pythagoras himself. Perhaps it doesn't matter. We do know that the Pythagorean school changed the way mankind perceived and used numbers and mathematics. Today, we put the school's theories to use in practical ways. In fact, almost every scientific field uses higher mathematics: astronomy, engineering, computer science, medicine, architecture, and physics, just to name a few.

FYI
For Your Info

The Cradle of Democracy

Each ancient Greek city-state had its own government. By the sixth century BCE, when Pythagoras lived, many were ruled by dictators or tyrants. These were usually aristocrats who managed to gain control by winning the support of the common people. Although they were in control, they really had no legal right to rule.

Philip of Macedon

Early in the sixth century BCE, a lawyer named Solon became popular when he urged Athenians to fight for the island of Salamis. The Athenians won and Solon became a hero. At his urging, Athenians began to take more interest in their government. He wrote new laws that made life for the common man better. Debtors were no longer sold into slavery to pay their debts. The poorest class, the Thetes, were allowed to vote for the first time, although they still couldn't hold political office.

The Spartans helped overthrow Athens' last tyrant, Hippias, in 510 BCE. A radical politician and aristocrat named Cleisthenes established democracy.

The truth is, the Athenians weren't as democratic as we'd like to think. Only free men could vote. Women, slaves, and foreigners, even Greeks from other city-states, could not. At the time, Athens was an empire that ruled many city-states. The citizens in Athens proper voted, but citizens in other city-states under Athenian rule did not.

In the fourth century BCE, Philip of Macedon conquered all of Greece, including the democratic Athens. He allowed the Athenians to control their local communities, but he still ruled as their king. In 146 BCE, Greece became a province of the Roman Empire. Over a thousand years later, the Normans took over. The Turks made Greece a part of the Ottoman Empire in 1453 CE. Greece gained its independence from Turkey in the war of 1821–1829 and joined the European Union in 1981.

Chronology

(by tradition)

BCE

566 Buddha is born.

560 Pythagoras is born on the Greek island of Samos.

542 Pythagoras travels to Miletus to study with Thales and Anaximander.

538 Pythagoras travels to Egypt to study.

525 Pythagoras is exiled to Babylon after Persians invade Egypt.

512 Pythagoras returns to Samos and starts first school, the Semicircle.

518 Pythagoras starts new school at Croton, in southern Italy.

508 Pythagorean school is attacked and destroyed during uprising against Pythagorean society. Pythagoras dies.

450 Second revolt throughout southern Italy against Pythagorean society.

Timeline
in History

BCE	
3400	Egyptians use straight lines to represent values.
3000	Egyptians use hieroglyphic numerals.
	The abacus is used in the Middle East.
1800	Babylonians know Pythagorean Theorem.
1200	Trojan War
1000	Greeks colonize the eastern coasts of the Aegean Sea.
800	Greeks adopt the Phoenician alphabet.
776	First Olympic Games.
750–700	Homer writes the *Iliad* and the *Odyssey*.
753	Rome is founded.
660	Greek man named Byzas founds town of Byzantine.
597	Babylonian King Nebuchadnezzar destroys Jerusalem.
539	Cyrus the Great of Persia conquers Babylon.
508	Democracy begins in Athens.
480	Persians defeat Greeks in Battle of Thermopylae.
472–410	Greek theater thrives.
462–429	Age of Pericles
460	Hippocrates, Greek "Father of Medicine," is born.
450	Greeks use written numerals.
447–432	Greeks build Parthenon in honor of the goddess Athena.
431–404	Sparta defeats Athens in Peloponnesian Wars.
399	Socrates is executed.
356	Alexander the Great is born.
146	Rome conquers Greece.
100	Chinese are the first to use negative numbers.
47	Julius Caesar captures Alexandria, Egypt; the Great Library of Alexandria burns.

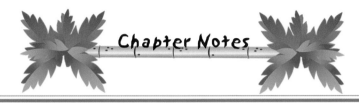

Chapter Notes

Chapter One: An Age of Genius

1. Iamblichus, *On the Pythagorean Life*, translated by Gillian Clark (Liverpool, England: Liverpool University Press, 1998), p. 3.

2. Margaret Wertheim, *Pythagoras' Trousers: God, Physics, and the Gender Wars* (New York: Times Books, 1995), p. 3.

3. J. A. Philip, P*ythagoras and Early Pythagoreanism* (Toronto: University of Toronto Press, 1966), p. 186.

4. Wertheim, p. 20.

5. Philip, p. 188.

6. Ibid.

7. Ibid.

8. Ibid.

9. Ibid., p. 190.

10. Ibid.

11. Wertheim, p. 22.

13. Walter Burkert, *Lore and Science in Ancient Pythagoreanism*, translated by Edwin L. Minar Jr. (Cambridge, Massachusetts: Harvard University Press, 1972), p. 110.

Chapter Two: The Pythagorean School

1. Margaret Wertheim, *Pythagoras' Trousers: God, Physics, and the Gender Wars* (New York: Times Books, 1995), p. 22.

2. G. S. Kirk, J. E. Raven, and M. Schofield, KRS. *The Presocratic Philosophers, 2nd ed.* (Cambridge, Massachusetts: Cambridge University Press, 1983), pp. 226–227.

3. Hobart Huson, *Pythagoran: The Religious, Moral and Ethical Teachings of Pythagoras* (Refugio, Texas: self-published by author), p. 197.

Chapter Three: Pythagorean Philosophy

1. Kenneth Sylvan Guthrie, *The Pythagorean Sourcebook and Library: An Anthology of Ancient Writings Which Relate to Pythagoras and Pythagorean Philosophy* (Grand Rapids, Michigan: Phanes Press, 1987), p. 71.

2. Arnold Hermann, *To Think Like God: Pythagoras and Parmenides, the Origins of Philosophy* (Las Vegas, Nevada: Parmenides Publishing, 2004), p. 31.

3. Margaret Wertheim, *Pythagoras' Trousers: God, Physics, and the Gender Wars* (New York: Times Books, 1995), p. 34.

4. Ibid., p. 35.

5. Ibid., p. 36.

Chapter Four: The Essence of All Things Is Numbers

1. Margaret Wertheim, *Pythagoras' Trousers: God, Physics, and the Gender Wars* (New York: Times Books, 1995), p. 30.

2. Ibid., p. 25.

3. Ibid., p. 10.

4. Ibid., p. 26.

Chapter Five: His Final Years

1. *Margaret Wertheim, Pythagoras' Trousers: God, Physics, and the Gender Wars* (New York: Times Books, 1995), p. 24.

2. Arnold Hermann, *To Think Like God: Pythagoras and Parmenides, the Origins of Philosophy* (Las Vegas, Nevada: Parmenides Publishing, 2004), p. 69.

3. Ibid., p. 85.

4. Ibid., p. 86.

5. Wertheim., p. 10.

6. Ibid., p. 10.

7. Ibid., pp. 4–5.

Further Reading

For Young Adults

Hakim, Joy. *The Story of Science, Book One: Aristotle Leads the Way*. Washington, D.C.: Smithsonian Books, 2004.

Karamanides, Dimitra. *Pythagoras: Pioneering Mathematician and Musical Theorist of Ancient Greece*. New York: Rosen Central, 2006.

Suplee, Curt. *Milestones of Science*. Washington, D.C.: National Geographic, 2000.

Works Consulted

Burkert, Walter. *Lore and Science in Ancient Pythagoreanism*. Translated by Edwin L. Minar Jr. Cambridge, Massachusetts: Harvard University Press, 1972.

de Vogel, C. J. *Pythagoras and Early Pythagoreanism: An Interpretation of Neglected Evidence on the Philosopher Pythagoras*. Netherlands: Van Gorcum & Co., 1966.

D'Olivet, Fabre. *Golden Verses of Pythagoras*. New York: G. P. Putnam's Sons, 1917.

Fauvel, John, Raymond Flood and Robin Wilson (editors). *Music and Mathematics: From Pythagoras to Fractals*. Oxford, England: Oxford University Press, 2003.

Gorman, Peter. *Pythagoras: A Life*. London: Routledge Kegan & Paul, 1978.

Guthrie, Kenneth Sylvan. *The Pythagorean Sourcebook and Library: An Anthology of Ancient Writings Which Relate to Pythagoras and Pythagorean Philosophy*. Grand Rapids, Michigan: Phanes Press, 1987.

Hermann, Arnold. *To Think Like God: Pythagoras and Parmenides, the Origins of Philosophy*. Las Vegas, Nevada: Parmenides Publishing, 2004.

Huson, Hobart. *Pythagoras: The Religious, Moral and Ethical Teachings of Pythagoras*. Refugio, Texas: self-published by author, 1947.

Iamblichus. *On the Pythagorean Life*. Translated by Gillian Clark. Liverpool, England: Liverpool University Press, 1998.

Kahn, Charles H. *Pythagoras and the Pythagoreans: A Brief History*. Indianapolis: Hackett Publishing Company, 2001.

Kirk, G. S., J. E. Raven, and M. Schofield. *The Presocratic Philosophers, 2nd ed.* Cambridge, Massachusetts: Cambridge University Press, 1983.

Navia, Luis E. *Pythagoras: An Annotated Bibliography*. New York: Garland Publishing, 1990.

O'Meara, Dominic J. *Pythagoras Revived: Mathematics and Philosophy in Late Antiquity*. Oxford, England: Clarendon Press, 1989.

Philip, J. A. *Pythagoras and Early Pythagoreanism*. Toronto: University of Toronto Press, 1966.

Riedweg, Christoph. *Pythagoras: His Life, Teaching, and Influence*. Translated by Steven Rendall. Ithaca, New York: Cornell University Press, 2002.

Wertheim, Margaret. *Pythagoras' Trousers: God, Physics, and the Gender Wars*. New York: Times Books, 1995.

On the Internet

Ancient Greece http://www.ancientgreece.com

BBC: *Ancient Greece Timeline* http://www.bbc.co.uk/schools/ancientgreece/timeline/index.shtml

History Link 101: *Ancient Greece* http://www.historylink101.com/ancient_greece.htm

Kidipede—History for Kids: *Ancient Greece* http://www.historyforkids.org/learn/greeks

MATHGYM: *Pythagoras of Samos: A Collection of Essays and Lessons for Junior and Senior High Students* http://www.mathgym.com.au/history/pythagoras/pytheor.htm

PBS: *The Greeks: Crucible of Civilization* http://www.pbs.org/empires/thegreeks

School of Mathematics and Statistics/University of St. Andrews, Scotland: *Mathematicians Born Before 500 AD* http://www-groups.dcs.st-andrews.ac.uk/~history/Indexes/_500_AD.html

Glossary

archetype	(AHR-kih-typ)—A pattern or model.
aristocrat	(uh-RIS-tuh-krat)—A person of noble birth.
aqueduct	(AA-kwih-dukt)—A man-made channel for moving water over long distances.
algebra	(AL-juh-bruh)—A higher branch of mathematics that deals with relations between numbers.
arc	(AHRK)—A curved line.
astronomy	(ah-STRAH-nuh-mee)—The science of explaining the behavior of matter in outer space.
city-state	(SIT-ee-STAYT)—One of the independent cities in ancient Greece.
circumference	(ser-KUM-frunts)—The distance around a circle.
consonance	(KAHN-suh-nunts)—A combination of sounds occurring at the same time that produce a pleasing sound.
cosmos	(KOZ-mohs)—The universe; an orderly system.
cremate	(KREE-mayt)—To burn a dead body.
cult	(KULT)—Any religious system that requires great devotion.
cuneiform	(kyoo-NEE-uh-form)—An early numbering and writing system based on symbols.
dictator	(DIK-tayt-er)—A ruler with absolute power.
disciple	(dih-SY-pul)—A student or follower.
divine	(dih-VYN)—Of or pertaining to a god; godlike.
enigma	(uh-NIG-muh)—Something that can't be explained; a puzzling occurrence of story.
geometry	(gee-AH-mah-tree)—A higher branch of mathematics that measures shapes; literally means "earth-measurement."
mystical	(MIS-tih-kul)—Pertaining to the spirit.
novice	(NAH-vis)—Someone who is new to something.
octave	(OK-tuv)—The set of eight notes that make up a musical scale.
oracle	(OR-ah-kul)—A priest or priestess in ancient times through whom the gods were believed to speak.
parable	(PAIR-uh-bul)—A story that teaches a truth, usually religions or moral.
philosophy	(fih-LAH-suh-fee)—The study of truths and principles of knowledge.
ratio	(RAY-shee-oh)—The comparison of two numbers.
reincarnation	(ree-in-kar-NAY-shun)—The belief that the soul doesn't die when the physical body dies, but instead inhabits a new physical body.
solstice	(SOHL-stis)—One of the two days each year during which the sun reaches it northernmost position in the sky.
transmigration	(tranz-my-GRAY-shun)—The passing of the soul from one body into another after the first body dies.
transpose	(tranz-POHZ)—To change the relative position or order.
unison	(YOO-nuh-sun)—At the same time.
zealot	(ZELL-ut)—A fanatic.

Index